GRACE
Inspired Power to Lead

Rabon (Ray) Coleman

Ray Coleman / VIP Leadership Institute
101 Bobwhite Drive
Dickson, TN 37055
Phone (800) 729-5206

Table of Contents

This book is dedicated to my mother, Lorene Coleman, with love.

My mother has inspired me throughout my life. She always told me that I could be or do anything that the mind could conceive. Mother taught me high moral and ethical standards which I have tried to uphold at all times.

"Be good to others, and they will be good to you." That is the slogan by which she has always lived. My mother has always had a heart of grace, so it is fitting that dedicate this book with love for her. Unfortunately, my mother passed away before this little volume was published, however, golden memories of her smile and graceful actions will never be forgotten by those for knew her.

Rabon (Ray) Coleman

PREFACE

This little volume is the result of both my personal experience and my good fortune of working with successful leaders who choose to lead with Grace. I have worked with many Graceful leaders, but I have also experienced disgraceful people who foolishly believed they were leaders. It is the latter that I hope to affect in the current culture of out organizations. I certainly recognize a need for a positive shift.

The original title to this book was "Power to Grow". However, after reviewing a HBR blog about the death of leadership pioneer Warren Bennis, I chose to change the title of my book. Warren Bennis contributed a lifetime to leadership by being an author, teacher, and advisor. Warren's last interview with HBR indicated that his next book would be one word, "Grace". Unfortunately, "Grace" never made it to the bookstore shelves. However, those who knew him had the privilege of knowing the contents of the book through their encounters with him. I chose to change the title of my book to "Grace" to honor Warren's life and contribution to leaders everywhere.

New successful leaders will have to possess "Grace" in order to listen, understand, and project a higher quality of leadership. It is my desire that this book will acquire this and motivate people to take graceful actions.

GRACE
Inspired Power to Lead

Book I

Choosing to Lead with Grace

Grace is a word that you rarely find in leadership books. Yet, when it is applied, any organization can be inspired to greatness. No family, organization, or nation has ever achieved greatness without a great leader. Today, our society and institutions are searching for motivation and are constantly seeking leaders who can change the culture for the better.

Leadership is a great responsibility.

In the business world owner and stockholders are demanding more return on their investments. Consumers want lower prices along with better quality and immediate delivery. Employees want a workplace where they matter and have a voice. I believe that the only way we can achieve these results is by applying the concept of grace to our workplaces.

Employees, in particular, control the atmosphere and potential success of a company.

When employees have hope for the future, they will possess power for the present which will result in a more successful organization. An effective leader brings out this power within their employees by embracing grace and playing to their strengths while not focusing on weaknesses. Those who choose to lead with grace, love to lead, love their followers, and embrace the positive results that are achieved though implementing graceful leadership.

> "Power isn't control at all - power is strength, and giving strength to others. A leader isn't someone who forces others to make him stronger, a leader is someone willing to give is strength to others that they may have strength to stand on their own."
> - Beth Revis

1

There will be a chapter devoted to each of the five Graceful Leadership principles:

G - Gratitude

R - Respect

A - Action

C - Compassion

E - Emotional Intelligence

When you apply grace to your leadership style, a new culture is created within your organization. This new culture requires getting the employees involved in the change process. Managers and employees need common goals and priorities to form a strong work culture. Tell them what needs to change and ask them how it can be done together, as a team. By getting the employees involved in the beginning stages, change and growth occur within the employees comfort zone.

Who is responsible for the culture of your organization?

Within organizations, we find persons responsible for sales, quality, manufacturing, purchasing, etc. Who is directly responsible for the culture in your organization?

> "The leaders who work most effectively, it seems to me,   never say 'I'. And that's not because they have trained themselves not to say "I".   They don't think "I" They think "we"; they think "team". They understand their job to be to make the team function. They accept responsibility and don't sidestep it, but "we" gets the credit. This is what creates trust, what enables you to get the task done."
> - Peter F. Drucker

No one person can do everything on his own. Someone has to focus on the development of the work missions and make sure thing are moving in the right direction. Focusing on the culture should be a priority in any organization. If the employees are using words like "they" or "them" and not "we" or "us", then beware: there will be problems in your future.

Build your organization with people who want to give 100% and add value to your organization. Graceful leaders want their employees to succeed and live up to their maximum human potential. They can achieve this potential by leaders effectively communicating the beliefs and values of the company inside and outside of the organization. Employees must fully understand the culture of the workplace and it must fit in with what is important to them. Reward and recognize those who advance the culture within the company. A graceful culture will greatly influence the people you attract and retain. The way is set by the graceful leader who makes sure everyone is working together as a team.

"A true leader is responsible for his followers who have reposed their faith in his leadership. If an ordinary man fails, it is a personal failure. But when a leader fails, he shatters the entire ideologies, principles, and morale of all those who followed him. The impact is much bigger and stakes are higher."

- Awdhesh Singh

Leadership is a great responsibility - and a privilege.

Leadership is a great opportunity to add value to an organization employees, businesses, and customers. We can elevate our culture by becoming more graceful, respectful, compassionate, and kind. We have people in supervisory and management positions that have never been taught the basic, fundamental art of dealing with other people. Owners of businesses need to understand that ROI is not only "return on investment", but also "return on individual". We need to invest in training, mentoring, and inspiring our management team. This can be achieved through the implementation of the principles of grace.

Grace is, in a way, just common sense leadership. Using these principles raises· morale, increases creativity, and connects all the people together into a winning team. Applying grace breeds positive energy. The voices of the workers are heard, and the graceful leader listens. Within the GRACE principles are contained the keys to genuine job satisfaction. Employees discover hope for the future.

GRACE is giving up self for the sake of others.

It is in building relationships that achieve amazing, desired results. Organizations that offer GRACE for their workers care about them as people, value their contributions, and can expect the best of the people they employ.

If your actions inspire others to dream more, learn more, do more and become more, you are a leader."   -John Adams

Leading with the Grace of Gratitude

*"As we express our gratitude, we must never forget the highest apprecia-
tion is not to utter words, but to live by them."*
John F. Kennedy

When gratitude is practiced in the workplace, relationships improve and the staff is more effective. A culture of gratitude creates a happier work environment. Employees are more considerate of others needs and more appreciative of what others contribute. The workers have increased energy, performance, and focus along with being more loyal to the business and the company and themselves more. When we elevate our attitude and take positive actions to create a culture of hope and gratitude, we inspire others to do the same.

We say "thanks" in our homes, stores, and schools, but we fail at saying "thanks" in the workplace. With a majority of experts in the management field agreeing that grateful leaders are more likely to succeed, one would think that common courtesy would be prevalent within the workplace, but it is not. This is despite the fact that "thank you" at work makes the employees feel good, appreciated and motivated.

I am reminded of a story. As Jesus was traveling along the border between Samaria and Galilee, he passed by a group of ten men on the outskirts of a village. The men were all suffering from leprosy, and when they spotted Jesus they called out to him "Jesus, Master, have pity on us!" Jesus saw them and said "go show yourself to the priest." The men followed his command and were made clean. One of the group, a Samaritan foreigner, upon noticing that he was healed, came back to praise Jesus. Jesus asked the man "Were not all ten cleansed? Where are the other nine? Was no one found to return and give praise to God except this foreigner?"

"All business and jobs depend on a vast number of people, often unnoticed and unthanked, without which nothing really gets done. They are all human and deserve respect and gratitude."
- Margaret Hefferman

In the workplace, we have many managers and employees who are like the nine who did not practice gratitude. We are actively suppressing gratitude at work and even robbing ourselves and others of grace. Without gratitude, we are just real estate or equipment. Today's management teams just do not say "thank you" enough. Even our business schools do not put an emphasis on gratitude. However, grateful leaders do emphasize their gratitude for their employees, and are rewarded with positive thinkers and productive workers.

Without gratitude, a disease of negative thinking develops. Complaining is constant and everyone blames everyone else for their failures.

Do you have a grateful work environment? Do co-workers and management show simple acts of appreciation at work through saying "thank you" or compliments? Saying "thanks" is showing others that you care about them and that their contributions are sincerely appreciated. Thanking the employees and showing appreciation for their commitment to achieving greater performance requires little effort and does not cost the company a dime.

> "It's a sign of mediocrity when you demonstrate gratitude with moderation."
> - Roberto Benigni

Gratitude can have an impact on the bottom line decreasing customer complaints, increasing productivity, and decreasing absenteeism. In addition, the behavior that is rewarded (gratitude) will be repeated, thus having an endless positive ripple effect. The action of gratitude can serve to build communication, responsibility, and collaborations amongst co-workers, thus creating a dynamic team that turns their values into profits for their company. And they will look forward to going to work each day.

It feels great to thank and be thanked. It is reported that gratitude has a whole host of health and psychological benefits including: better sleep, lower levels of anxiety and depression, and a more positive outlook on life. Grateful people have a higher level of life satisfaction, optimism, and a greater level of positive emotions. They achieve more and possess a greater sense of responsibility toward social issues and others.

By showing gratitude you are more engaged in the workplace. Giving
is a motivating emotional process. Grateful leaders get results. So, why
are we still waiting to engage grace and gratitude in our organizations?
What is keeping you from becoming a successful, grateful leader?

Our workplaces are the worst place to find examples of gratitude and
grace. Some people even consider gratitude to be "soft" management.
The only truth in this belief is that the absence of gratitude creates "soft"
profits, low productivity, and an undesirable workplace. When people are
motivated, it makes them want to contribute more. Gratitude is available
to everyone, costs nothing, and drives the organization forward. Gratitude
is contagious.

All gratitude requires is paying attention to the people, their dy-
namics and performance, and supporting them while also letting them
know that, their work matters. If it is so easy, why is it missing in our
workplaces? Many things contribute to the lack of gratitude including:
management that is too busy being busy, untrained or under trained management and supervisors, and a lack of understanding of the power of
gratitude. In many cases, the management just cannot connect the dots
between the act of gratitude and the increase in profits and productivity.

Gratitude is a very powerful attribute with which we can improve
leadership, productivity, and teamwork in the workplace. We need to encourage each other to be the best that we can be. The true value and
power of any organization is the grace and gratitude that is generated
through its relationships. We have to consider the relationships with our
staff, vendors, customers, and outside community.

Leading with Respect

"If you have respect for people as they are, you can be more effective in helping them to become better than they are."

- John W. Gardener

Respect is a top priority for graceful leadership. Employees want to be treated with dignity and respect. They want to be recognized for their individual contributions to the organization. Turnover of personnel in the workplace is tied directly to the lack of support and respect from management and organizational leadership. When workers feel disrespected, they feel as if their work is not important or noticed. The usefulness of an employee greatly depends upon the extent to which respect is practiced by the leadership and organization.

As leaders, we reveal our true character through our communications and actions. Leaders are called leaders because they are to be first; they are intended to set the standard.

A true leader's character includes honesty, respect, gratitude, compassion, and a powerful vision for the future. These effective qualities of a leader will inspire the team and stimulate productivity in the workplace. You cannot be an effective leader if you do not have respect for those you lead. Remember-: in order to get respect, you must first give respect.

> "When people honor each other, there is a trust established that leads to synergy, interdependence, and deep respect. Both parties make decisions and choices based on what is right, what is best, what is valued most highly."
> - Blaine Lee

There are many leadership skills needed in order to gain respect. Listening to others is one of these necessary skills. When a leader listens to an employee, the employee feels more empowered and valued within the organization. The best leaders know how to keep personal problems confidential.

A good leader will not allow their employees to be disrespectful to each other. Disrespectful employees should be removed from the team.

However, a good leader who is full of respect for his employees will inspire that same level of respect amongst the workers.

Leadership is about people. The true task of a leader is to encourage people and have them follow your lead on their own volition. Respectful leadership is an action that develops self-determination within the employee. The employee and the leader can identify the group's vision together with respect. The organization can achieve greater improvement in performance through respectful and graceful interaction. Respectful leadership includes respect for the employee's work and for the employee as a person.

> "Surround yourself with the best people you can find, delegate authority, and don't interfere as long as the policy you've decided upon is being carried out"   - Ronald Reagan

Being the leader does not always mean that you have earned the job. Many leaders take for granted their position or title and sometimes think that they are owed respect because of their spot in the organizational chart. Sitting in the ivory tower or corner office does not display a leader's level of competency. A respectful leader is not afraid of getting his hands dirty through "hands-on" work. The greatest leaders are not afraid to take risks, set the standard, and give credit to the team.

A better knowledge of grace, respect, gratitude, and compassion could enable any leader to have a major break-through and affect a major change in their team and company.

Leadership is about teaching and leading people, not machines or things. When leaders treat their team with great respect and care, the performance of the company gets better. When the employees feel disrespected by the leaders they will never fully invest themselves in the mission or goals of the organization. Highly respected employees will go the extra mile and give 110% of themselves to achieve the leader's objective.

> "Leaders who win the respect of others are the ones who deliver more than they promise, not the ones who promise more than they can deliver."   - Mark A. Clement

In order to grow your organization, you must have leadership that has the ability to inspire, motivate, and engage people into creative, considerate, and desired actions. In today's competitive marketing environment, we need people to step up and be aggressive. We need people to be good thinkers and strong leaders who can drive our companies forward. And, one cannot forget about the human side. We need gracious leaders NOW! What actions are you taking to make things happen?

Actions of a Graceful Leader

"All companies of any size have to continue to push to make sure you get the right leaders, the right team, the right people to be fast acting, and fast moving in the marketplace. We've got great leaders, and we continue to attract and promote new leaders." - Steve Ballmer

ACTION is what makes leaders successful. It is action that produces results such as developing others, building relationships, and making decisions leading to more effective actions. The actions of the leader and their teams, along with the positive outcomes that they produce, will build the reputation of a great and successful leader and his company.

Deciding when to take action, and what type of action to take, is the choice of leadership. Building the right team for the proper task is a high priority of a leader. One of the first responsibilities of a leader is to communicate their visions to the employees. This will ensure the leader a higher level of success. A leader can create desirable results by creating a desirable environment.

Actions are triggered by decisions and continued decisions are needed for continued actions. Leadership is not a popularity contest, and there will certainly be times when the leader makes unpopular decisions. However, it is in the best interest of all concerned that the right action be decided.

> "Great leaders communicate a vision that captures the imagination and fires the heart and hearts of those around them."
>
> -Joseph B. Wirthlin

A good leader needs the mind, ears, and heart to lead with the action of grace. To a confident leader, there is no challenge too big to handle. Once you adopt the right attitude with the right choices, the employees will follow suit and every challenge will present a new opportunity for greater achievement.

To be a strong leader you have to unlock the inner potential of the employees to become greater individuals. Your employees are like a garden.

Give them care. Get rid of the weeds. They will produce and take care of your needs.

Many people wonder how leaders know when to make the right decisions. The decision making process comes from an accumulation of lifetime experiences. Many senior leaders say that they depend on their gut feelings when making decisions.

However, it is actually a combination of their experiences, emotional intelligence, and their understanding of the power of grace in their decision making process that makes them superior at making the right decisions.

Great leaders need to communicate regularly and openly in order for the team to realize their goals and visions for the organization. Employees need to know their importance in making things happen.

Great leaders inspire their followers into action. It may be difficult for some leaders to master all leadership traits. Most leaders are strong in certain areas and weak in others. Once the employees notice the leader is practicing the new traits or making a change for the better, the employees will follow them.

> "Leadership is an action, not a position."   - Donald McGannon

Here are some actions and traits that make up a good leader. My hope is that you will master them and become a leader of grace and action.

1. **Trustworthy** - Be honest and the employees will know where you stand.
2. **Respect** - They will not respect you if you don't respect them.
3. **Passion** - A leader has passion and uses it to drive the team forward and ignite others to action.
4. **Vision** - Leadership success always starts with a vision. The vision provides a sense of direction- a route to the future.
5. **Confidence** - You must believe in yourself as a leader.
6. **Compassion** - Employees want to be treated fairly, understood, appreciated, and trusted. The new breed of leaders use compassion effectively.
7. **Values** - The values and ethics of a leader should be visible in your actions every single day. Actions speak louder then words.

8. **Communication** - great leaders share their vision and strategy with the team they lead.
9. **Gratitude** -Say "Please" and "Thank You" more often and be more appreciative of the team you lead.
10. **Responsibility** - Take responsibility for your actions and the actions of the team.
11. **Inspiring** - Leaders inspire people to reach great heights of performance and success. Their passion and purpose play lead roles in making a great leader.
12. **Compliments and Praise** - Make people feel important - because they are.
13. **Decisive** - Make things happen by not putting off decisions.
14. **Accountability** - Take full responsibility when the team fails regardless of where mistakes were made.
15. **Listening** - The employees have a voice and need to be heard. Be a good listener.
16. **Fairness**-People will respect a leader who is tough as long as he is fair.
17. **Care** - Great leaders care about the company, and they also care about the workers who make the company run like a clock.
18. **Empowering** - Great leaders encourage their employees and make them feel powerful.
19. **Humor** - Great leaders do not take everything seriously. They want their followers to find joy and humor and use these attributes to elevate the human spirit.
20. **Engagement** - Leaders offer challenges, seek employee's ideas, and recognize employees for their contributions.

"In the end, it is important to remember that we cannot become what we need to be by remaining what we are."

-Max De Pree

Leading with Compassion

"The act of compassion begins with full attention, just as rapport does. You have to really see the person. If you see the person, then naturally empathy arises. If you tune into the other person, you feel with them. If empathy arises, and that person is in dire need, then empathic concern can come. You want to help them, and then that begins a compassionate act. So, I'd say that compassion begins with attention." - Daniel Goleman

Compassion is rarely found in the workplace or in leadership books. However, the time has come to change. Great leaders inspire people with hope, purpose, energy, and optimism. Our organizational cultures are ready for a change, but it is going to take compassionate leaders to make that happen.

Driving the people, instead of leading them, produces stress within the workforce. Stress causes a multitude of health problems. Couple that with the toxic emotions caused by uncompassionate leaders and you have a costly stew that is damaging to the culture and company as a whole.

Stress causes employees to lose focus, energy, and their sense of connection to the organization and its people. Prolonged periods of toxic emotions caused by stress leads to employee turnover, loss of innovation, unproductive employees, poor customer service, and disappointing bottom-line results.

> "Too often we underestimate the power of a touch, a smile, a kind word, a listening ear, an honest compliment, or the smallest act of caring, all of which have the potential to turn a life around."
> - Leo Buscaglia

We must adopt a leadership style that can strengthen our relationships and create a more supportive and less stressful workplace. A compassionate leader can transform the most challenging workplaces. When the leader chooses compassion and is seen as a kind person, the employees start to notice and connect.

Compassion can be present in the workplace each day through simple acts of kindness. Leaders can offer compliments and words of encouragement because, after all, the employees want to work with a leader who honestly respects them, their values, and their contributions. A productive workplace where employees want to work is created by leaders who practice kindness and compassion.

Understanding compassion is to serve the needs of others. We have to help others before we can expect them to help us. Go the extra mile and do unexpected kindnesses. Incorporate kindness into your leadership and watch where it can take both you and your company.

In order to be compassionate, you have to be interested in what makes people tick. You can develop a strong relationship with people by simply asking about their interests.

> "Loving-kindness and compassion are the basis for wise, powerful, and sometimes gentle, and sometimes fierce actions that can really make a difference - in our lives and those of others."
> - Sharon Salzberg

Here is a touching story about a young man who worked at a local factory. He had clocked in late on several occasions over a ninety day period, which was cause for suspension from the job. The young man had mentioned to his supervisor and the human resources director that he had to drive over a hundred miles one-way each day to see his ill mother, who has in hospice care. One day, the president of the company called the young man into his office. The man just knew that he was going to be suspended from his job. Once he had entered the office and taken a seat, the president asked "How is your mother?" As the young man broke down in tears. The president showed his compassionate leadership by saying "Anything that you need, we are here for you."

Along the same theme as the previous story is the tale of Brandon Cook of New Hampshire and his cancer-stricken grandmother. When the grandmother was unable to eat the hospital soup, Cook sought out her favorite clam chowder from the local Panera Bread Company restaurant. Unfortunately, the store was not making that soup on that day. The manager of the store was moved by Mr. Cook's plight and had the soup made especially for his ailing grandmother. They even included a box of fresh baked cookies as a gift from the staff.

> "The more you care, the stronger you can be." -Jim Rohn

Compassion is not a sign of weakness; it is a sign of strength. It is a sign that you care about people. Compassion is power with the people. Compassion and kindness come from a deep place within-the heart. Compassionate leaders lead by example, manage their emotions productively and openly, and are aware of the effect of their words and actions on employees. We need to recruit and retain leaders with grace, respect, and gratitude.

Emotional Intelligence:
Characteristic of a Great Leader

"Emotional intelligence is a way of recognizing, understanding, and choosing how we think, feel, and act. It shapes our interactions with others and our understanding of ourselves. It defines how and what we learn, it allows us to set priorities; it determines the majority of our daily actions. Research suggests it is responsible for as much as 80% of the 'success' in our lives." — J. Freeman

Most effective leaders today have a high degree of emotional intelligence. Emotional intelligence is the ability to identify, access, and control the emotions of oneself, others, and groups. Daniel Goleman, author and psychologist, identified the chief components of emotional intelligence as self-awareness, self-regulation, motivation, empathy, and social skills. Goleman found direct correlations between emotional intelligence and measurable business results.

Imagine a leader that is thought to be low on empathy by his subordinates. The leader is unable to properly listen or react to his staff. The lack of emotional intelligence would have a negative impact on the company's overall performance. This leader would find that changing his emotional intelligence would require a major effort and strong determination.

Choosing to lead with grace (gratitude, respect, action, compassion, and empathy) is a great start towards becoming a great leader that is effective in any workplace.

> "75% of careers are derailed for reasons related to emotional competencies, including inability to handle interpersonal problems; unsatisfactory team leadership during times of difficulty or conflict; or inability to adapt to change or elicit trust."
> — The Center of Creative Leadership

The first area of emotional intelligence is self awareness. Self-awareness is having a serious understanding of your strengths, weaknesses, emotions, personal requirements and purpose. Leaders with self-awareness are honest with themselves and with their co-workers.

Self-regulation is the impulse that drives our emotions. Leaders that are in control of their impulses and feelings are able to create an environment of fairness and trust. Business is full of change today. In order to grow and compete, we have to be productive and effective. The leaders with self-regulation are more effective in dealing with change in the workplace.

Motivation is a skill possessed by all effective leaders. Leaders with this trait are driven to excel and achieve beyond expectations. These leaders have the drive, energy, and passion to achieve high levels of performance. Motivation relates to strong leadership and raises the bar of success.

Empathy in leadership takes into consideration the employee's feelings and emotions and is essential in making intelligent decisions. Empathy plays a major role in retaining and developing good people. Being empathetic to those within your organization produces better relationships and performance.

Leaders must have the ability to manage relationships with and of others. The goal should be moving people in a direction that is desired by the organization.

In today's world, there are many distractions and stresses that prevent us from being the best we can be. We must reframe out perspectives and use our emotional intelligence to deal with issues as they arise. A leader's ability to identify, perceive, and manage emotions will provide the basis for the kind of emotional and social abilities that are required for success in almost all jobs.

Your emotional intelligence is just as important as you intellectual ability, or IQ, when dealing with people. It is not always the smartest people who are the most successful. The world is full of bright people, however, the social skills of grace, listening, and empathy are still lacking in many workplaces. Your emotional intelligence will determine your effectiveness at managing relationships, leadership, and job performance.

"Tenderness and kindness are not signs of weakness and despair, but manifestations of strength and resolution."

- Kahlil Gibran

Building a Workplace with Trust and Grace

"Being trustworthy is something you are, something you stand for, and a core value to live by. It isn't something you can train for, nor is it something you can manipulate. You either have those values or you don't."
-D. Nixon

Trust is a very important ingredient in graceful leadership. It is very difficult for an organization to grow if the leaders are not trustworthy. However, you must first give trust before you can receive it. Trust is built over time by consistently exhibiting values, integrity, and other graceful actions. Trust is timeless and also timely, but it can be lost if you place blame for your failures on others, including subordinates.

Trust is an essential principle of grace within an organization. Loss of integrity is a strike against the leadership of any group. Damage to trust can negatively impact growth, productivity, and profits. Employees that distrust their leaders are more likely to be engaged in less positive behavior.

Most people will agree that trust is the most important element in successful organizations. When the employees trust their leaders, they are more engaged and have higher efficiency rates.

> "I never trust an executive who tends to pass the buck. Nor would I want to deal with him as a customer or supplier."
> - James Cash Penney

One of the factors that causes mistrust in the workplace is the lack of communication from the owners / managers to the employees. When decisions are made by management that affect the employees, those employees need to know why those decisions were made. The employees want to be part of and recognized by the organization. Therefore, do not overlook the impact of effective communication. Openness and honesty are needed in today's workplaces. Be honest and trusting and you will earn others trust and honesty.

The leaders must set standards and examples for employees to follow. The workers appreciate when management can own up to their mistakes. We are all human and far from perfect. Sometimes we are going to fail and make mistakes. Acknowledging those mistakes will go a long way towards earning the trust and respect of employees. Mutual trust will grow the business and its people.

Building trust takes time and starts at the top of the organization. Integrity is critical in building trust in any relationship. The management sets the vision for the company, and are responsible for communicating the plan, direction, and vision to the employees. By building trust and grace in the workplace, we can create an environment of high trust that will increase innovation, creativity, and a greater commitment to achieving desired results.

> "Surround yourself with people of integrity, and get out of their way. In my adult years as a manager, Bob Galvin, the former CEO of Motorola, was my most influential leader. He told me, 'a good leader knows he is doing a good job when he knows with certainty that he can say yes to anything his staff asks and feel totally confident that they will do the right thing.' If you surround yourself with the people who have integrity, and they understand well the goals and objectives of the organization, then the best thing to do as a leader is to get out of their way. I use this advice quite a bit at work. The right people will feel more pressure to perform well when they are trusted."
>
> - Hector Ruiz

Senior leaders need to place a high value on trust and integrity. They also have to communicate to all member of the organization effectively. Trust is the emotional element that connects the leaders and followers together. Senior leaders must establish cultures where trust exists throughout the organization. The leaders need to be vocal and also visible on building trust. The graceful leader must make certain that they articulate a compelling vision, set high standards of expectation, and actively demonstrate personal commitment and enthusism. They also should show interest, personal support, and confidence in their employees and the overall organization.

Sowing Seeds of Grace
Reaping Leadership Benefits

In order for a workplace to expand and thrive, good leadership must be a top priority. The organization, regardless of its size, needs to teach leadership practices and leadership skills. A skilled business and its organizational leaders are able to achieve the goals and improve the overall performance of the employees. When new and emerging managers are properly trained in leadership and management skills, there is an immediate increase in confidence and performance. The increased performance is recognized both within the organization and by the customer.

Leadership training and development are key components in improving and growing any business. A key role for the leader is to inspire, engage and motivate the staff, create great customer service, and push the team to exceed expectations.

When we sow seeds of grace in the workplace, the benefits of leadership are immediately recognized. The leaders inspire and motivate the staff to stretch themselves on important projects. Leaders enable the business to develop deeper and more trusting relationships with the workers and the customers. The graceful leader nurtures a company culture that creates retention and loyalty. Enthusiasm is created by leaders through times of difficult change and challenges.

When graceful leadership is present in an organization, it can be felt throughout the entire organization. The company culture is not forced by good leaders; it is developed by them.

Under graceful leadership, everyone understands the vision and goals of the organization and everyone is valued for their contribution. The employees feel that they are an important part of the company and that their jobs matter. Employees are encouraged to do their very best and understand that helping their co-workers to succeed is the best way for all to get ahead and be a winning team. Graceful leadership produces high morale, great employee performance, and sustainable long-term achievement.

Effective leadership is the key to success in any size of business. An effective leader must master the art of teamwork. The leader recognizes that all the members of the team are important to achieving the company's objectives and should be treated with respect and rewarded accordingly.

With grace, your ethical standards in business should be constant and above reproach at all times. The entire organization benefits from the high ethical standard that the graceful leader influences those around him to have on a daily basis.

When we sow seeds of gratitude, the benefits are numerous. Gratitude affects our careers, health, social standing, personality, and emotions. The career benefits include better management, goal achievement, and improved networking. The social benefits include kinder, deeper relationships, more friendships, etc. One's health benefits via improved sleep, less illness, and greater longevity. The personality benefits are a more optimistic outlook, less self-centeredness, decreased materialistic tendencies and increased self-esteem. The emotional benefits are being more relaxed, improved mood, and greater resiliency. There is reason to believe that gratitude can extend your lifespan by a few months or even years.

So, what is blocking you from sowing seeds of gratitude and receiving the harvest of leadership?

Sowing the seeds of respect can change the course of your life. When you have respect for others; others will have respect for you.

Leadership and career opportunities can come to you by simply sowing the seeds of respect. When showing respect, your reputation is enhanced and others feel respected and treated well in your presence. Practicing respect to the workplace enhances your skill set in the minds of the staff and workers. The workers feel more valued in your organization when you show them respect in the presence of others.

Opportunities to express compassion and sow the seeds of compassion are greater now than ever before in history. There is so much change that can be made through personal acts of caring, kindness, and support of others. WARNING: compassion is contagious and can spread throughout the workplace. Compassion enables you to understand yourself and others better as you seek to ease the unpleasant circumstances of co-workers. Compassion opens your heart and enlarges your perspective as you consider others needs and problems. You are better connected in your relationships by practicing compassion towards those who surround you.

The key to developing compassion in your life is to sow seeds of compassion daily. In this way, it becomes a part of your grace in leading others. By sowing the seeds of grace daily, you can change somebody's life-perhaps even your own. You can change lives, the direction of your company's culture, and leave a legacy that can be modeled by others in the workplace.

GRACE
Inspired Power to Lead

Book II
Short Stories of Leadership

Leadership: A Gift
By Robert "Bob" Goosman

Caring Is An Everyday Action for Leadership
By Ned Southerland

The Local Liberia Connection
By Jim Curry

My Dad Was No Leader, But My Neighbor Was
By Bob Isbell, M.A.

Leadership Thoughts Into Words
By Perry Hamlett

The Best Deal in Town
By Mary F. Lame

The Contributors

Robert "Bob" Goosman lives in retirement in Florida after years of living in Cincinnati. He was considered the leading expert in the field of making and distributing material handling containers. He was welcomed in all of the Fortune 500 companies.

Ned Southerland has lived in his beloved Tennessee river country his entire life. Known to all as "Cornbread Ned", he has inspired countless audiences with tales of his selling days. His motto is: That which I am to be I am now becoming.

Jim Curry was born and raised in Savannah, Georgia and returns there every year for St. Patrick's Day. He lives in Pegram, Tennessee and is a popular writer of world history and sports topics.

Bob Isbell lives in Kingston Springs, Tennessee. An Army veteran, he is a leading life insurance underwriter in Middle Tennessee. But his first love is coaching his two sons in baseball and soccer and martial arts.

Perry Hamlett is the principal broker of one of the largest real estate companies in Tennessee. He devotes his every activity to the love of God. This faith has made him a compassionate and graceful leader.

Mary F. Lame is retired and lives in Nashville with her husband. She has authored several books and publications on faith based subjects. She is admired as a thorough researcher. Her story in this book is evidence of her ability to inspire with words.

Leadership: A Gift
By: Robert (Bob) Goosman

How does one obtain the role of a leader? Does it come from God? Does it come from others? Does it come from experience? Yes to all three!

A true leader must have moral principles. Leaders that use lies, force, threats, and intimidation are not true leaders. They are imitators and rarely do they succeed over a long period of time. Their dishonesty will show up and it will be their demise. A true leader recognizes that God's law of loving your neighbor as yourself must be a given in anything that he or she accomplishes.

A good leader is smart, and being smart, recognizes that other people are smart and that they can be a great asset to his or her success as a leader. Sometimes there can be one outstanding person who can, by their actions, greatly influence a good leader. One such an example was Ronald Reagan. He came to be a great leader of our country. He was warm and friendly, and yet, decisive and demanding. He had no formal training in the political arena, but soon after taking office, he had the politicians eating out of his hands and listening to his every word. How? He surrounded himself with good, honest, hardworking people whom he trusted. He led them, but did not suppress them. He recognized their talents and he supported them. He was a people person and a religious person who remembered God's law.

All leaders have failed at one time or another. Leadership requires risk. In all risk there is an element of win or lose. Show me a leader who has not failed, and I will show a bad leader. It is out of those failures that the real leader emerges. It teaches humility and it teaches courage. From failures come success in a true leader. Let's call it experience.

In my case, my leadership plan was based upon God, my employees and friends, and my experiences. I do not know if I was a successful leader, but I do hope that my employees, my investors, and my God received a fair return on their investment.

Caring is an Everyday Action For Leadership
By: Ned Southerland

"The tragedy of life is not that we die, but rather what dies inside a man."
　　　　　　　　　　　　　　　　　　　　- Albert Shweitzer

I am convinced that the greatest fear of most people is being rejected. When someone acts out, whether child or adult, it is most often a cry of "please notice and accept me". When rejected, they get angry, they act up in some way. When they act up, they feel guilty. With guilt comes rejection, which starts the cycle all over again. They tend to reject others by rejecting their ideas and authority. The cycle must be broken. Good leadership qualities are necessary to break this cycle.

The story is told of a lady that dies, then she is given the chance to return to earth and relive just one day. When asked what day she would like it to be, she says, "Oh, I'd like it to be my 12th birthday". All the dead beg her, "Don't do it, don't do it". "But I want to see my Momma and Papa again", the lady said. So, she returns to that day and comes down the stairs in the pretty dress. But her mother is too busy making the birthday cake to notice. "Mom, look at me, I'm the birthday girl." "Fine, birthday girl", her mother answers, "sit down and eat your breakfast." The girl stands there on the steps and begs, "Mom, look at me!" But mom doesn't look. Then Dad comes through the house, but he doesn't look because he is too busy making money to buy her presents. And big brother, sure enough, does not look.

"Please, please will someone look at me? I don't need your cake, I don't need your money. Please just look at me - recognize me." Nobody looks. She turns and says "take me back, I forgot what it was like to be human".

Nobody looks at nobody, no one really cares, do they?

A successful, well trained leader will notice, they will care. Not only will they notice, they will use everyone's strength to overcome their weaknesses.

Often, good people are eliminated from a job when a little recognition and persistence will mean success.

Persistence is the single greatest factor to success in any field, especially leadership. Calvin Coolidge said it this way:

"Nothing in this world can take the place of persistence. Talent will not; nothing in more common than unsuccessful men with talent. Genius will not; unrewarded genius is almost a proverb. Education will not; the world is full of educated derelicts. Persistence and determination alone are omnipotent. The slogan 'press on' has solved and will always solve the problems of the human race."

Victor Borge, a well-known humorist, tells the story of his uncle who wanted to invent a new soft drink. He worked all night on a formula until finally at 4 o'clock he thought he had it. He called it 4-up. It was a failure. The next night again, he worked all night finishing at 5 o'clock. He called it the 5-up. Again, it was a failure. The third night, he worked again all night until 6 o'clock and name it 6-up. Again, he failed. He gave up and quit. What a shame he never knew how close he came.

Stories like above make it clear that it's always too early to quit. "What a shame" Borge would say with a laugh, he never knew how close he came.

Much research has been done on people who live on skid row. They found that those people come from different backgrounds and circumstances. There is a lot they don't have in common. However, the one thing that all share is that they've given up on life. Press on.

It is not so much a questions on how much hope we have, but in what we hope. I think often of the story in the Bible where the rich young ruler came to Jesus telling of all his goodness and his riches, but was wise enough to ask Jesus the question "what lack I yet?"

It is a questions we all should ask ourselves. Especially those who have become leaders. "What do I lack?" Where is my hope founded?

For further review, may I suggest that we should always work to develop integrity, that is doing the right thing for the right reasons.

The Local Liberia Connection
By: Jim Curry

The tragic epidemic of the deadly Ebola virus, spreading throughout western Africa has put the spotlight on the republic of Liberia. The fear of Ebola spreading worldwide has dominated radio and TV news. Liberia has taken its place beside Ukraine and Syria as places NOT to visit. Folks from Kingston Springs and White Bluff may have felt a peculiar feeling when they hear Liberia mentioned so often. If so, here's why, Read on.

Following the War of 1812, a group of southern farmers organized a movement to free Negro slaves in America and return them - no matter how many and no matter the cost - to Africa. In 1821 these white farmers, out of sheer compassion and human love, sent a Methodist minister, Jehudi Ashmun, to west Africa. The movement, now named the American Colonization Society (ACS) appointed a spokesman who would coordinate their mission with the Rev. Ashmun. This spokesman purchased 38,000 square miles along the Atlantic Ocean. By 1824 the surveys were completed and the boundaries were confirmed. They named this new country Liberia... Latin for "free land". They name the capital Monrovia in honor of President Monroe. The first shiploads of the freed slaves were called America - Liberians. The indigenous native Africans did not immediately take to the newcomers, but the Methodist church labored (as they always do) and soon everybody became friends and family. English became the main language. Christianity flourished.

Thousands of slaves were freed and returned to Liberia over the next thirty (30) years. These southern farmers of the ACS did not need a war or an act of Congress to give freedom to these slaves. They were motivated by God's love.

I told you the name of the minister who went to Africa, but I failed to give you the name of the spokesman for the ACS who planned the mission and who raised all the enormous sum of money to complete the mission. He was out very own Montgomery Bell. He is considered the co-founder of Liberia.

Let us hope that Liberia can find a person like him today.

My Dad Was No Leader,
But My Neighbor Was
By. Bob Isbell, M.A.

I'll be the first to admit that my Dad was not a leader. He never took and active role in the community, in youth sports, or in the church. Thus, very early in my life, I did not benefit from exposure to good quality leadership. I was at a neighbor's house when I was around 14 years old. I'll refer to my neighbor as "Bud".

I was throwing a baseball with Bud's son, and Bud commented on the velocity of my fastball as I whizzed a pitch into his son's catcher's mitt. Bud asked if my Dad had showed me how to throw a curve. I responded, "No, my Dad and I have never even played catch". Bud then said, "Bobby, I'm gonna teach you how to throw a curve that won't harm your arm, and you're gonna be able to throw it effectively in the next five minutes". "Do you believe me?" I said, "Yes Sir". I think I led the league in strikeouts the following season.

Bud gave me some additional confidence when I was age 16. Until that time, I had really never been in a leadership position. Bud asked me to be the assistant coach of his 13, 14, and 15 year old Babe Ruth Baseball team. I was concerned that I would not have enough time to contribute to the team, because I was playing high school baseball, worked on a farm, and was attempting to keep up with my school work. Bud said, "I have confidence in you, and we'll try to work around your busy schedule". I agreed to help him. About half way through the season, Bud announced that he was going to retire from his coaching position on condition that his assistant coach, Bobby Isbell, be named as the new head coach. I went on to coach that Babe Ruth team for the next three years with success each season.

Bud is only one example of many leaders who have given me opportunities throughout the years. Bud, however, showed me what an opportunity looks like.

My Leaderships thoughts put into words

These few simple examples sum up my leadership philosophy that work well for me. Jesus Christ is my leader.

When Jesus was asked, "Of all of the commandments, which is the most important?" He answered, "Love the Lord your God with all your heart and with all your soul and with all your mind and with all your strength. The second is this, Love your neighbor as yourself. There is no commandment greater than these."

In business I believe that:

"The customer is my most important visitor.
He is not dependent on me. I am dependent on him.
He is not an interruption of my work. He is the purpose of it.
I am not doing him a favor by serving him,.
He is doing me a favor by giving me the opportunity to serve him."

I believe that a leader should have a leader to follow. Everyone can be a leader no matter where they are in life. A leader should serve those that he or she is blessed to lead. Whether you are holding the door open for someone or managing a company, always lead by example wherever you are and strive to be better everyday!

Perry Hamlett, Principal Broker
The Realty Association
"Dedicated to a Standard of Excellence"

The Best Deal in Town
By: Mary F. Lame

Sarah Hightower turned on the television set so her children could watch their favorite cartoon shows. This was the only entertainment they could afford. Money was extremely tight for this single mother of two.

The TV blared on and a commercial for used cars appeared, "Baby have I got a red hot deal for you," said the salesman. He was showing a shiny, bright red convertible. "Can't you just see yourself behind the wheel in this fabulous machine? Come on down to Big Hal's Used Car Lot on Main Street today. We are the only used car dealer in town that gives you 90 day guarantee on all of our cars, and fills her up with a full tank of gas before you leave with the car of your choice. If your car ever breaks down, I will have it hauled back to our lot and refund your money in full with no questions asked. Come on in, I look forward to meeting you and doing business with you."

Sarah knew that the commercial was probably a lot of hype, but she knew she would have to purchase a car soon. She had been late to work 3 times in the last month, and her boss told her if she could not get to work on time she would have to let her go. She was taking the bus to work, and had missed it twice, but the third time was not her fault; the bus broke down and they had to send a replacement. The bus broke down and made her two hours late for work. Her boss was ready to fire her then, but Sarah asked her to call the bus line and verify the breakdown.

Sarah had been saving to buy a new car out of her meager wages, but she had to dip into the car fund several times for the sake of her children, seems like the car fund was always getting lower and lower. She was glad she could pay the bills that kept coming. She was remembering the warnings that she had heard about used cars, and used car dealers. She was feeling desperate, she did not want to lose her job; she needed the income to keep up the family. After much vacillating back and forth she arrived at Big Hal's Used Car Lot. She was looking over the rows of cars when Big Hal appeared.

"You're in the wrong place, little lady, you need to check out our daily specials first; the red hot deals are on the other side of the lot."

She followed Big Hal to a row of nice looking cars. She saw the price on one of the cars and her heart sank. She knew she could not even buy one of these fairly new used cars as they were almost the price of a new car.

"I'm sorry, I'm just wasting your time. I can't afford any of these cars," said Sarah.

"What did you need a car for, Mrs. Hightower?" Asked Big Hal.

"I need it for my job, to get to and from work. I had been taking the bus, and missed it on several occasions; and I thought a car might be more reliable," said Sarah.

"Oh, you are really in luck today. I have The Working Girl's Special, let me show it to you. At least give it a try; I am sure we could work out a reasonable payment plan for you," said Big Hal.

He took her over to a brown, medium sized sedan. The body style was not classy by any means; it was simple and plain. She did not see any price listed on the car.

Big Hal said, "Let's take her out for a spin. You will love how she handles on the road; she's as smooth as silk on those curves."

Sarah got in the driver's seat and started the engine. The engine had a nice hum to it; at least it was not sounding like an old clunker. They drove down to the end of town and out onto the highway.

"Do you have any little ones at home?" asked Big Hal?

"Yes, I have two small children, Jason 7, and Melissa 4," said Sarah. "I was just thinking that the backseat would be perfect for children, lots of room back there. You could put both children and several bags of groceries back there," said Big Hal.

"How much do you want for this car?" asked Sarah.

This car was the worse color that Sarah could have envisioned a car being, not to mention the body style was plain and humdrum. She was waiting for Big Hal to inform her that she could not afford to buy it anyway, because her car fund didn't have enough money in it.

Big Hal and Sarah pulled back in the car lot and he said to her, "Mrs. Hightower, I have a soft spot in my heart for working mothers. My Mama was a working mother. She raised 8 of us children, and she always told me to help our any working mother I could. So here is the best deal I can possibly offer you. I am going to have my mechanic look over the car one more time just to be sure it is in tip top shape. I will give you a 120 day guarantee and sell it to you for this price. He showed Sarah his note pad that had $100 less that her car fund had in it.

"Thank you so much Big Hal. I don't know how I can ever repay you," said Sarah.

"Oh, you must pay, or I will repossess the car," smiled Big Hal.

"That is not what I meant, I mean for giving me the "Working Girl's Special," said Sarah.

"I will be paid well; I will keep your business for a lifetime. You and your family will love Big Hal. Your two little ones would not think of letting anyone but Big Hal put them in their first car. I can see it now, 'The First Time Car Buyers Special,' when little Jason takes the wheel and rolls out of here in his new car going to work, or when little Melissa goes off to college in her sporty new 'Pretty Girls' Special'. Once you do business with Big Hal you don't ever go anywhere else." Said Big Hal.

Sarah learned something important from Big Hal that day. What you want, and what you think looks good, might not be what you need. What you need may be something entirely different than what you envision in your mind. If Sarah had not been willing to take what she needed in place of what she wanted; she could have been waiting and struggling for those things that were going to be out of her reach for a very long time. She learned how to be content with that which she had and could afford on that day, and every day thereafter.

The children screamed when she drove home and parked the car in the driveway. "Wow, a brand new car! We love it, Mom!" They both jumped into the back seat and yelled, "Let's go for a ride!"

She was driving the children around town. She turned onto Main Street and realized they would be passing Big Hal's Used Car Lot. The children said, "Look, there is Big Hal. Hey, Big Hal," they yelled at the top of their lungs.

Big Hal gave them a big wave and a thumb's up sign. "Yes, there go three very satisfied customer," he thought.

He walked over to a young couple with a small baby in tow and said, "Have I ever got a deal for you, 'The First Time Homebuyers Deal.' You said you just bought your first home, and need a real bargain; with your new house and young one here. Here it is right here. He pointed to a blue sedan. This car was owned by an old lady that only drove it church once a week. Runs like a top. Let's take it for a spin, you'll love it."

The baby squealed and threw his pacifier in the air. Yes sir, Big Hal was winning over some more satisfied customers. Yes, people that were short on cash and wanted high quality used cars were pouring in.

After all, Big Hal had the secret: good used is good to be used. He made sure that only good, used cars were on his lot. He learned a lot from

Mable Goodall who ran the local flea market. Her motto was: "If your stuff ain't any good for you, it won't be any good for me, or anyone else either. Bring only good used items in here to sell. You can give the rejects to your mother-in-law for Christmas."

The admiration that Big Hal had for Mable showed over the receiving door in his garage: "If it ain't a good used car, don't even drag it in here, I don't want it, the junk yard across town is waiting for you."

Sarah Hightower took comfort in these two signs and the two individuals that ran these businesses. She felt privileged to live in a town where quality was part of the fabric of everyday life. Looking at Big Hal and Mable Goodall she wanted what they had. She struggled and planned, and changed her profession. She changed her vocation to sales also. She became a real estate salesperson.

Do you need a modestly priced house (good, or used, or both)? Sarah is the go-to agent that can place you in a home you can afford. She will take you over to preview the house in her slightly used car, negotiate a reasonable price, and take a picture of you and your family in front of your new / used house on the date of possession with her used camera from Mable's flea market. Sarah has specialized in the small home buyer. She is known not only to see young families get homes, but that they also get used furniture, or a used car from two very old and dear friends of hers. This is one of the reasons she won top in sales for this year. She has a lot of people helping her behind the scenes. For instance, the Business Man of the Year (Big Hal), who gives her his "Best Deal in Town" advice, and Mable who gives her inside information on what is coming up in the next flea market that a young couple struggling to make ends meet could use.

Honesty, high standards, good quality, and a genuine desire to help others obtain something they need (used or new) is a sure formula for success in sales. Everyone must buy the salesman first (what he is saying about his product), or they will never buy the product he is selling. If the salesman turns out to be false, or the product he is selling turns out to be worthless, the customer will probably never use either one of them again.

Mable inspired Big Hal, Big Hal inspired Sarah, and Sarah inspires us all. Live up to the highest level of expectations for yourself and success will follow you. Try to put yourself in the people's shoes that you serve, and see his needs, and how you can fulfill them. Sure you are in the game to make some money, and you will. Remember dollars are just a few figures on a sheet of paper. When you are gone, not one will remember how much money you were worth, but how much you helped others will never be forgotten by them, or by the town that you lived in. The legacy you leave will be your life, not your money, or your latest commission figures.

The three people in this story were not in sales for the money; they were in sales to serve other people's needs. They all prospered well and made plenty of money, but the money was never their motivation, service to their fellow man was. Helping others was their first priority. So the money came in second place, but it came to them just the same.

It never bothered the town folks that Big Hal drove a used, vintage Corvette, that was his motto, "Good / Used", the car cost a small fortune, but who cares? Big Hal deserved the best used car there is, because he gave the best he had to a town full of modest used car buyers.

Mable Goodall had a house full of antique furnishings worth a king's ransom, but who cares? She spent her life making sure everyone in town had the same chance to get a good price on good / used antique furnishings for their homes.

Last, but not least by any means, is Sarah. She and her two children just moved into a large antebellum mansion at the edge of town. How did she get the money for this marvelous, large home? Maybe a huge bonus from her real estate company for salesperson of the year? No, the little old lady that owned the property was a friend of her late grandmother. Mrs. Fletcher wanted to leave the house to Sarah because she admired the person that she was, and knew she would always take good care of her home. She knew that Sarah was a good person, and that her family had always been thoughtful of others. She wanted her to have a good place to bring up her children in; in a town that they both loved. Mrs. Fletcher had a large estate and her family all lived out of state and they did not need the house. Sarah had seen the large house several times of the years, but it never occurred to her that one day the house would be hers. She had been so busy trying to get small home buyers the best deal in town that she had neglected trying to get a good / used house for herself. It looks like someone was making sure that she got the best deal in town this time. Who was that? Just maybe it was the person who owns the real title and deed to the property that we live on. We only have a lifetime lease. It looks like we own property but don't. All Mrs. Fletcher was doing was transferring her lifetime lease over to Sarah; after Mrs. Fletcher talked to the real owner and made sure she was doing the right thing.

GRACE
Inspired Power to Lead

Book III

Selected Quotes On Leadership

"Not the cry, but the flight of a wild duck, leads the flock to fly and follow."

- Chinese Proverb

"Leaders must be close enough to relate to others, but far enough ahead to motivate them."

- John C. Maxwell

"Leadership is the capacity to translate vision into reality."

- Warren G. Bennis

"Leadership is not about titles, positions, or flowcharts. It is about one life influencing another."

- John C. Maxwell

"It is better to lead from behind and to put others in front, especially when you celebrate victory when nice things occur. You take the front line when there is danger. Then people will appreciate your leadership."

- Nelson Mandela

"Leaders aren't born, they are made. And they are made just like anything else, through hard work. And that's the price we'll have to pat to achieve that goal, or any goal."

- Vince Lombardi

"The challenge of leadership is to be strong, but not rude; be kind, but not weak; be bold, but not bully; the thoughtful, but not lazy; be humble, but not timid; be proud, but not arrogant; have humor, but without folly."

- Jim Rohn

"The very essence of leadership is that you have to have a vision. It's got to be a vision you articulate clearly and forcefully on every occasion. You can't blow an uncertain trumpet."

- Reverend Theodore Hesburgh

"Never tell people how to do things. Tell them what to do and they will surprise you with their ingenuity."

- General George Patton

"The key to successful leadership today is influence, not authority."

- Kenneth Blanchard

"I start with the premise that the function of leadership is to produce more leaders, not more followers."

- Ralph Nader

"Lead and inspire people. Don't try to manage and manipulate people. Inventories can be managed but people must be lead.'

- Ross Perot

"Management is efficiency in climbing the ladder of success; leadership determines whether the ladder is leaning against the right wall."

- Stephen Covey

"Earn your leadership every day."

-Michael Jordan

"You don't lead by hitting people over the head - that's assault, not leadership."

- Dwight Eisenhower

"Where there is not vision, the people perish."

- Proverbs 29:18

"Keep your fears to yourself, but share your courage with others."

- Robert Louis Stevenson

"As we look into the next century, leaders will be those who empower others."

- Bill Gates

"There is no persuasiveness more effectual that the transparency of a single heart, of a sincere life."

- Joseph Berber Lightfoot

"One of the tests of leadership is the ability to recognize a problem before it becomes an emergency."

- Arnold Glasow

"A good general not only sees the way to victory; he also knows when victory is impossible."

- Polybius

"A great leader's courage to fulfill his vision comes from passion, not position."

-John Maxwell

"I must follow the people. Am I not their leader?"

- Benjamin Disraeli

"A leader is a dealer in hope."

- Napoleon Bonaparte

"You gain strength, courage, and confidence by every experience in which you really stop to look fear in the face. You must do the thing you think you cannot do."

- Eleanor Roosevelt

"'Never give an order that can't be obeyed."

- General Douglas MacArthur

"The first responsibility of a leader is to define reality. The last is to say thank you. In between, the leader is a servant."

- Max DePree

"A true leader has the confidence to stand alone, the courage to make tough decisions, and the compassion to listen to the needs of others. He does not set out to be a leader, but becomes one by the equality of his actions and the integrity of his intent."

- General Douglas MacArthur

"To do great things is difficult; but to command great things is more difficult."

- Friedrich Nietzsche

"Lead me, follow me, or get out of my way."

- General George Patton

"Our chief want is someone who will inspire us to be what we know we could be."

- Ralph Waldo Emerson

"A good leader is a person who takes a little more than his share of the blame and a little less than his share of the credit."

- John Maxwell

"A leader takes people where they want to go. A great leader takes people where they don't necessarily want to go, but ought to be."

- Rosalynn Carter

"Great leaders are not defined by the absence of weakness, but rather by the presence of clear strengths."

- John Zenger

"All of the great leaders have had one characteristic in common: it was the willingness to confront unequivocally the major anxiety of their people in their time. This, and not much else, is the essence of leadership."

- John Kenneth Galbraith

"Outstanding leaders go out of their way to boost the self-esteem of their personnel. If people believe in themselves, it's amazing what they can accomplish."

- Sam Walton

"A good objective of leadership is to help those who are doing poorly to do well and to help those who are doing well to do even better."

- Jim Rohn

"A ruler should be slow to punish and swift to reward."

- Ovid

"Before you are a leader, success is about growing yourself. When you become a leader, success is all about growing others."

-Jack Welch

"To command is to serve, nothing more and nothing less."

- Andre Malraux

"He who has great power should use it lightly."

- Seneca

"What you do has far greater impact than what you say."

- Stephen Covey

"Just because something isn't a lie does not mean that it isn't deceptive. A liar knows that he is a liar, but one who speaks mere portions of truth in order to deceive is a craftsman of destruction."

- Criss Jami

"Alone we can do a little; together we can do so much."

- Helen Keller

"To have long term success as a coach or in any position of leadership, you have to be obsessed in some way."

- Pat Riley

"A good plan violently executed now is better than a perfect plan executed next week."

- George Patton

"No man will make a great leader who wants to do it all himself, or to get all the credit for doing it."

- Andrew Carnegie

"My own definition of leadership is this: The capacity and the will to rally men and women to a common purpose and the character which inspires confidence."

- General Montgomery

"He who has learned how to obey will know how to command."

- Solon

"The final test of a leader is that he leaves behind him in other men, the conviction and the will to carry on."

- Walter Lippman

"Leaders think and talk about the solutions. Followers think and talk about the problems."

- Brian Tracy

"True leadership is guiding others to success. In ensuring that everyone is performing at their best, doing they are pledged to do and doing it well."

- Bill Owens

"Power isn't control at all - power is strength, and giving that strength to others. A leader isn't someone who forces others to make him stronger; a leader is someone willing to give his strength to others that they may have the strength to stand on their own."

- Beth Revis, Across the Universe

"A great person attracts great people and knows how to hold them together."

-Johann Wolfgang Von Goethe

"Leadership is the art of getting someone else to do something you want done because he wants to do it."

- General Dwight Eisenhower

"I am reminded how hollow the label of leadership sometimes is and how heroic followership can be."

- Warren Bennis

"The greatest leaders mobilize others by coalescing people around a shared vision."

- Ken Blanchard

"Leadership and learning are indispensable to each other."

- John F. Kennedy

"Authenticity is the alignment of head, mouth, heart, and feet - thinking, saying, feeling, and doing the same thing- consistently. This builds trust, and followers love leaders they can trust."

- Lance Secretan

"We know that leadership is very much related to change. As the pace of change accelerates, there is naturally a greater need for effective leadership."

- John Kotter

"Simplicity is the ultimate sophistication."

- Leonardo DaVinci

"A man who wants to lead an orchestra must turn his back on the crowd."

- Max Lucado

"The leader has to be practical and a realist yet must talk the language of the visionary and the idealist."

- Eric Hoffer

"Never doubt that a small group of thoughtful, concerned citizens can change the world. Indeed it is the only thing that ever has."

- Margaret Mead

"The growth and development of people is the highest calling of leadership."

-Harvey Firestone

"Leadership is a potent combination of strategy and character. But if you must be without one, be without the strategy."

-Norman Schwarzkopf

"When I give a minister an order, I leave it to him to find the means to carry it out."

-Napoleon Bonaparte

"So much of what we call management consists in making it difficult for people to work."

- Peter Drucker

"Don't necessarily avoid sharp edges. Occasionally they are necessary to leadership."

- Donald Rumsfeld

"A nation will find it very hard to look up to the leaders who are keeping their ears to the ground."

- Sir Winston Churchill

"If one is lucky, a solitary fantasy can totally transform one million realities."

-Maya Angelou

"We live in a society obsessed with public opinion. But leadership has never been about popularity."

- Marco Rubio

"Whatever you are, be a good one."

- Abraham Lincoln

"Management is about arranging and telling. Leadership is about nurturing and enhancing."

-Tom Peters

 "Don't waste your energy trying to educate or change opinions; go over, under, through, and opinions will change organically when you're the boss. Or they won't. Who cares? Do your thing, and don't care if they like it."

- Tiny Fey, Bossypants

"You are good. But it is not enough just to be good. You must be good for something. You must contribute good to the world. The world must be a better place for your presence. And the good that is in you must be spread to others."

- Gordon B. Hinckley

"Education is the mother of leadership."　　　　　　- Wendell Willkie

"If you would not be forgotten, as soon as you are dead and rotten, either write things worth reading, or so things worth writing."

- Benjamin Franklin

"A competent leader can get efficient service from poor troops, while on the contrary an incapable leader can demoralize the best of troops."

- John J. Pershing

"Men make history and not the other way around. In periods where there is no leadership, society stands still. Progress occurs when courageous, skillful leaders seize the opportunity to change things for the better."

- Harry S. Truman

"Effective leadership is putting things first. Effective management is discipline, carrying it out."

- Stephen Covey

"The adventure of life is to learn. The purpose of life is to grow. The nature of life is to change. The challenge of life is to overcome. The essence of life is to care. The opportunity of life is to serve. The secret of life is to dare. The spice of life is to befriend. The beauty of life is to give."

- William Arthur Ward

"He who has never learned to obey cannot be a good commander."

- Aristotle

"There are three essentials to leadership: humility, clarity, and courage."

- Fuchan Yuan

"My father had a simple test that helps me measure my own leadership quotient. When you are out of the office, he once asked me, does your staff carry on remarkably well without you?"

- Martha Peak

"Good leadership consists of showing average people how to do the work of superior people."

- John D. Rockefeller

"You don't lead by pointing and telling people some place to go. You lead by going to that place and making a case."

- Ken Kesey

"The art of leadership is saying no, not saying yes. It is very easy to say yes."

-Tony Blair

"Become the kind of leader that people would follow voluntarily; even if you had no title or position."

- Brian Tracy

"I am endlessly fascinated that playing football is considered a training ground for leadership, but raising children isn't."

-Dee Dee Myers

"A leader is one who knows the way, goes the way, and shows the way."

- John Maxwell

"I had no idea that being your authentic self could make me as rich as I've become. If I had, I'd have done it a lot earlier."

- Oprah Winfrey

"Your most unhappy customers are your greatest source of learning."

- Bill Gates

"The best leader is the one who had sense enough to pick good men to do what he wants done, and the self-restraint to keep from meddling with them while they do it.

- Theodore Roosevelt

"Effective leadership is not about making speeches or being liked; leadership is defined by results not attributes."

- Peter Drucker

"It is absurd that a man should rule others, who cannot rule himself."

- Latin Proverb

"A cowardly leader is the most dangerous of men."   - Stephen King

"Leadership does not always wear the harness of compromise."

- Woodrow Wilson

"I suppose leadership at one time meant muscles; but today it means getting along with people."

- Mohandas Gandhi

"I would maintain that thanks are the highest form of thought, and that gratitude is happiness doubled by wonder."

- Gilbert K. Chesterton

GRACE
Inspired Power to Lead

This book was written for the leader who has purpose and wants to be valued by the people they lead. One must no longer be ordinary and effective; one must aim for greatness in our organizations and our personal lives.

For the past decade, author, Rabon (Ray) Coleman has researched the differences in great leaders. He found that leaders who lead with grace, gratitude, respect, and compassion are making a breakthrough in leading others.

By developing grace in your leadership style, you can change somebody's life, including your own. You can change lives, change the culture of the organization and develop greatness that can be modeled by others in the workplace.

Purchase this book today and start making a difference in your leadership It is your time to lead: take charge of your life today !

"The leadership instinct you were born with is the backbone. You develop the funny bone and the wishbone that go with it."

- Elaine Agather

"Leadership is unlocking people's potential to become better."

- Bill Bradley

"If you tell me, it's an essay. If you show me, it's a story."

- Barbara Greene

"A mediocre teacher tells. The good teacher explains. The superior teacher demonstrates. The great teacher inspires."

- William Arthur Ward

"If your actions create a legacy that inspires others to dream more, learn more, do more and become more, then, you are an excellent leader."

- Dolly Parton

"The most basic of all human needs is the need to understand and be understood. The best way to understand people is to listen to them."

- Ralph Nichols

"Individuals play the game, but teams beat the odds."

- SEAL Team saying

"The only way to do great work is to love the work you do."

- Steve Jobs

"Innovation distinguishes between a leader and a follower."

- Steve Jobs

"No man is good enough to govern another man without that other's consent."

- Abraham Lincoln

www.ingramcontent.com/pod-product-compliance
Lightning Source LLC
Chambersburg PA
CBHW071231220526
45468CB00002B/809